My Friend Salt

The **New England Coastal Wildlife Alliance (NECWA)** is a non-profit organization based in southeastern MA. Our mission is to better understand and protect coastal marine wildlife found in the waters off New England. All proceeds from the sale of this book will go to support NECWA's many projects and activities.

Projects include:

- **New England Basking Shark and Ocean Sunfish Project (NEBShark)**, a community-sighting network in the Gulf of Maine for basking sharks and ocean sunfish.

- **Marine Wildlife Research Program**, a project to study whales and other marine animals observed off Cape Cod.

- **Marine Wildlife Internship**, an internship program for upper high school, college, and graduate students.

To learn more about NECWA, check out these websites:
- www.necwa.org
- www.necwanews.blogspot.com
- www.nebshark.org
- www.facebook.com/NecwaNews
- www.twitter.com/NECWAorg
- www.Instagram.com/necwa

My Friend Salt

Story copyright © 2015 by Carol D. Carson.

Illustrations copyright © 2015 by Adam Whittier.

Published by the New England Coastal Wildlife Alliance

11 Clarence Soule Drive, Middleboro, MA 02346 - 2647

ISBN 978-0-9907162-0-4

i

This book is dedicated to our good friend and colleague, Dr. John Jahoda, Professor Emeritus of Biology at Bridgewater State University, Bridgewater, MA. Dr. Jahoda has studied many species of marine wildlife in the coastal waters of New England. When studying whales off Cape Cod, he has often had the good fortune of observing Salt and members of her family.

Dr. Jahoda is an outdoorsman, as well as an avid fisherman and hiker. Over the years, he has collaborated with NECWA on numerous research projects, including studies on humpback whales, sea turtles, basking sharks, and ocean sunfish. We thank Dr. Jahoda for his support of NECWA and his tireless efforts to save marine wildlife, protect habitats, and educate communities.

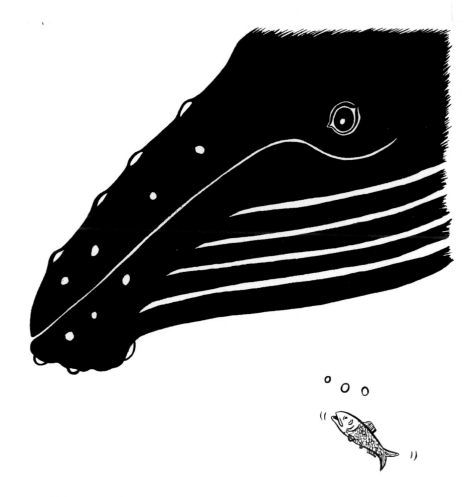

    I have a friend whose name is Salt. Having a friend like Salt is a bit unusual, for Salt is a humpback whale. Humpback whales are one of the largest animals that live in the ocean, yet these massive creatures are the gentle giants of the sea.

    In the spring, summer, and fall, Salt can often be found feeding in the waters off Cape Cod, MA. This gives me a chance to see her as I work as a naturalist aboard commercial whale watching boats. Often Salt will come over to our boat and spend time with us. These are my favorite moments out on the water.

    Each season, I look forward to seeing Salt and her growing family of humpback whales. Over the years, Salt has been a big part of my life and I consider her a good friend.

An adult humpback like Salt is close to 45 feet (13.7 m) long, which is the same length as a school bus! Salt and other females are often larger than the males and adults weigh close to 35 tons.

The tail of a whale is called the flukes. Salt's flukes are close to 15 feet (4.6 m) wide when measured from tip to tip. The large fin on Salt's back is called her dorsal fin. Each humpback whale has a dorsal fin with a unique size and shape.

The long front flippers are called the pectoral fins and they help Salt move gracefully through the water. Each fin is 1/3 the length of the body or 15 feet (4.6 m) long. The scientific name of the humpback whale is *Megaptera novaeangliae* and refers to the long pectoral fins for it means the "big-winged New Englander."

IT'S VERY DARK INSIDE A WHALE.

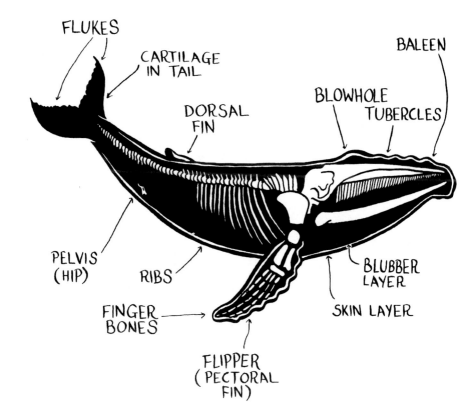

FLUKES
CARTILAGE IN TAIL
DORSAL FIN
BLOWHOLE
TUBERCLES
BALEEN
PELVIS (HIP)
RIBS
FINGER BONES
FLIPPER (PECTORAL FIN)
BLUBBER LAYER
SKIN LAYER

Only humpbacks have bumps called tubercles on their head and on the leading edge of each pectoral fin. Tubercles on Salt's head act like whiskers or important sensory tools. Tubercles on her pectoral fins help water move efficiently over each flipper.

Hidden inside Salt's large body is a flexible bony skeleton that provides structure and support. The bones that make-up the spinal column or backbone are called the vertebrae. That is why animals that have a backbone are called vertebrates.

All whales are mammals that give birth to live young and nurse their young with milk from mammary glands. Whales are able to stay warm in the cold ocean for they have a thick layer of blubber or fatty tissue under the skin that surrounds their body.

3

Like all mammals, Salt breathes air through her lungs. Salt's nose is called her blowhole and is located on the top of her head. Having her nose in this location helps Salt take a clean breath of air each time she comes to the surface.

When Salt breathes out or exhales, her warm and moist breath condenses as it mixes with the cooler ocean air above her. This creates a misty column that rises high into the air. Although Salt's blow will disappear within a few seconds, her forceful breath is visible miles from a boat or from the shoreline.

Scanning the horizon for distant blows using your eyes or binoculars is still the best way to find whales. This old whaling technique works better than any man-made instrument or tool.

Krill

Herring

Mackerel

Some of
Salt's favorite
things to eat.

American Sand lance

Each spring, Salt and other humpback whales migrate north to feast on krill and small schooling fish that are abundant in the cold waters of New England. Adult humpback whales eat close to 2 tons of food each day, which is about 4,000 pounds!

Salt is not a picky eater for she feeds on a variety of small fish that includes herring, mackerel, pollock, and menhaden. Her favorite food is the American sand lance, also called the sand eel, a pencil-sized fish found in the waters off Cape Cod.

It's hard to imagine that huge animals like Salt can survive on such small food or prey. Although these prey are miniscule in size when compared to Salt, krill and small fish are nutritious and provide a rich source of proteins and fats.

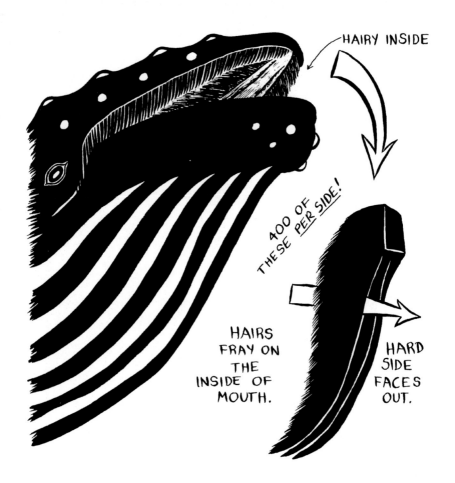

HAIRY INSIDE

400 OF THESE _PER SIDE_!

HAIRS FRAY ON THE INSIDE OF MOUTH.

HARD SIDE FACES OUT.

Salt and most large whales do not have teeth in their mouth. Instead, they have a hair-like material called baleen that grows down from the upper jaws. Whale baleen is flexible and durable as it is composed of a protein called keratin, which is also found in your skin, hair, and fingernails.

Baleen plates are triangular in shape and are arranged one beside the other like the teeth on a comb. Humpbacks can have up to 400 plates growing in series along the length of each jaw.

The inner edge of each plate has exposed hairs that create a frayed surface. The frayed edges of hundreds of plates combine to create a hairy mat inside the whale's mouth. Salt will use her baleen to strain or filter her food from the surrounding seawater.

PLEATS EXPAND
WHEN FEEDING

To capture tons of small-sized food each day, Salt and other humpbacks use a filtering technique called lunge feeding. As Salt lunges forward with her mouth wide-open, she scoops hundreds of gallons of food-filled seawater into her mouth and throat.

As seawater rushes into her open mouth, a series of grooves on the throat expand to increase the size of this enormous scoop. When her mouth is completely full, Salt closes her jaws and pushes the seawater back out in a process called straining.

Seawater can easily pass through the baleen hidden inside Salt's mouth. However, krill and small-sized fish are too large to squeeze through and become trapped inside. When all the water has been pushed out, Salt swallows her food whole! Yummy!

Salt uses a variety of filtering techniques when she feeds on different types of prey. When feeding on slow-moving prey like krill, Salt lunges slowly and often on her side. When feeding on fast-moving prey like small fish, Salt lunges aggressively and in an upright position. Salt must close her jaws quickly to prevent the fish from escaping out of her mouth.

When Salt feeds on agile fish like the American sand lance, she often blows nets of bubbles that help her corral her prey. As Salt encircles the school from below, she blows bursts of bubbles from her blowhole. This creates separate bubble columns that slowly rise to the surface and form a ring-like barrier around the fish. Bubble nets trap the fish inside, just like a fisherman's net.

The coastal waters off Cape Cod are part of a larger body of water called the Gulf of Maine. To the north of Cape Cod are two underwater banks called Jeffrey's Ledge and Stellwagen Bank. The presence of these shallow-water plateaus support a rich and productive environment that includes a diverse food web.

In 1992, the United States Congress decided to protect this important marine habitat by establishing the Gerry E. Studds Stellwagen Bank National Marine Sanctuary. This area is one of the largest national marine sanctuaries in the United States and protects 842 square miles of ocean at the mouth of Massachusetts Bay. The borders of this sanctuary include all of Stellwagen Bank, the southern portion of Jeffrey's Ledge, and surrounding waters.

NORTHERN GANNETS DIVING

HERRING GULL

ATLANTIC WHITE-SIDED DOLPHIN

HARBOR SEALS

GRAY SEAL

As winter approaches, Salt and the other humpback whales leave the cold waters of New England and head south to warmer, more tropical waters. The adults will migrate up to 1,500 miles to spend the winter in the Caribbean. Here, pregnant females give birth to babies called calves, and they raise their calves on their own. The other adults will spend time courting and mating.

Tropical waters are not as food-rich as colder waters to the north. This forces Salt and the other adults to fast for much of the winter. To survive, they will break down their blubber and use it as an alternate source of energy. Fasting is hard for adults and hardest for females who have recently given birth. These new moms use their blubber to keep themselves and their calves alive.

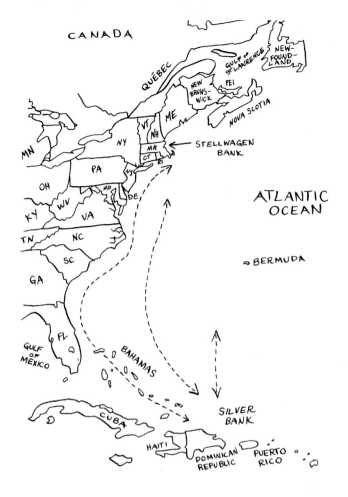

A humpback calf is between 10 to 15 feet long (3 - 4.5 m) at birth and weighs close to 1 ton. Newborns have a thin layer of blubber under the skin. Without this natural insulation, the calf must spend its first few months of life in warm, tropical waters.

Each day, the calf nurses from its mother and consumes close to 100 gallons of milk, which is rich in vitamins, proteins, and fats. This allows the calf to grow quickly in size and strength, and to develop the thick layer of blubber needed for colder waters.

By early spring, the adults and their calves will migrate north, back to the cold, productive waters of New England. It is now time for the adults to end their fast and feed once again on krill and small schooling fish, if they and their calves are to survive.

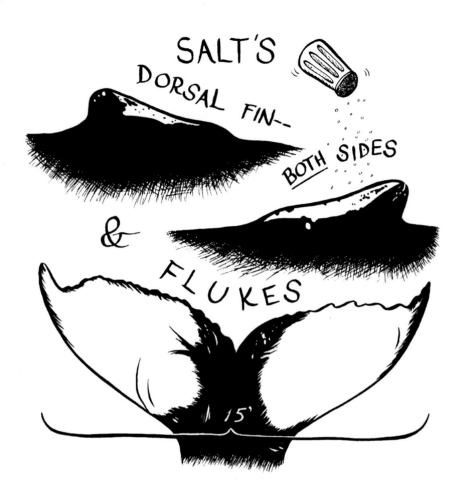

SALT'S DORSAL FIN--

BOTH SIDES

& FLUKES

15'

When humpback whales return to New England in the spring, biologists can recognize Salt and other individuals by looking at specific features and pigmentation patterns on their body. Each humpback has a unique size and shape to their dorsal fin. Salt's dorsal fin has a large amount of white pigmentation on the top, while other humpbacks have dorsal fins with scars and cuts.

A second identification feature is the ventral tail pattern, a beautiful black and white pattern on the bottom of the flukes. The ventral tail pattern can be seen when a humpback lifts its tail out of the water upon a deep dive. This pattern is created by variations in skin pigmentation and is unique to each individual. Therefore, the ventral tail pattern acts like a "fingerprint" for humpback whales.

SALT'S 13 CALVES

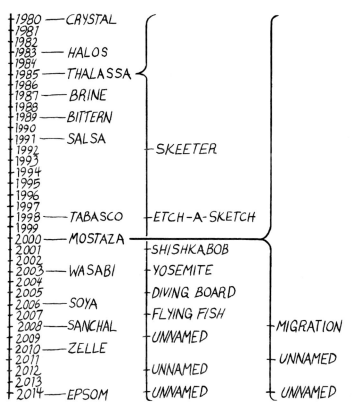

Salt was first seen as a young whale in 1976. She was the first humpback to be given a name by Captain Aaron Avellar, who ran a whale watch business from Provincetown, MA. He noted that the white scarring on the top of her dorsal fin made it look as if it had been "salted". The Avellar family continues the tradition of naming all of Salt's calves in their first year of life.

As of 2014, Salt has returned to New England with 13 calves. Like other humpback moms, Salt typically gives birth to a single calf every 2 to 3 years, and weans the calf within a year. Two of Salt's calves, Thalassa and Mostaza, have raised calves of their own. Their calves, and all other calves except Salt's, are named when they are a few years old by the researchers who study them.

When Salt and other humpback whales are seen offshore, researchers collect sighting information and photographs of each whale. Many of these photographs will be used to confirm the identity of the animal, while other photographs will be used in searchable catalogs called photo-identification catalogs.

Photo-identification catalogs, also called photo-ID catalogs, contain photographs of humpback whale dorsal fins or ventral tail patterns. A "dorsal fin catalog" organizes individuals by the size and shape of their dorsal fin. A "ventral fluke catalog" organizes individuals by the amount of black and white in the tail pattern. To make photo-ID catalogs easy to use, individuals with similar features are placed in the same section or area of the catalog.

FLUKE RANKING SYSTEM

| 1 | 2 | 3 | 4 | 5 |

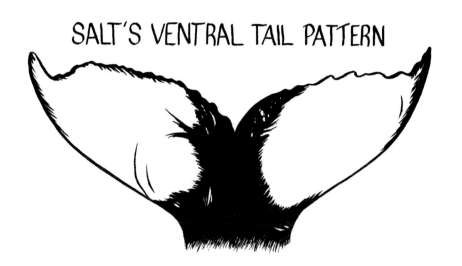

SALT'S VENTRAL TAIL PATTERN

Most ventral fluke catalogs use a number ranking system that is applied to the flukes. A mostly white tail pattern is ranked as a #1 fluke, while a mostly black tail pattern is ranked as a #5 fluke. Ventral tail patterns with various amounts of white to black are ranked accordingly, between the numbers 1 and 5. Using this ranking system, Salt's tail would be ranked as a #2 fluke.

The collection of sighting information and photographs for over 35 years has helped researchers better understand Salt and the life of the humpback whale. However, many questions remain unanswered. We don't know how many calves Salt or other adult females will have over their lifetime. We don't know how long Salt will live or the lifespan of any humpback whale.

Humpback whales are endangered worldwide as man has hunted this species to the brink of extinction. In 1986, the United States and most world countries agreed to ban all commercial whaling. Even so, the survival of whales and all marine wildlife is still threatened by many of man's activities.

Whales can be injured and sometimes killed when struck by boats, both large and small. Humans directly compete with whales for krill and small fish as man has overfished the oceans. Chemical and plastic pollution, as well as man-made noise in our oceans, impacts the health of all marine life. The effect of climate change, which includes rising ocean temperatures and ocean acidification, puts the health of the oceans and all who live in the oceans at risk.

WHAT CAN YOU DO?

Here are some fun and easy ways to help keep our oceans and all their inhabitants safe, healthy, and productive.

Reduce - Reuse - Recycle (the 3 R's)

Make the 3 R's a part of your daily routine. We all need to reduce what we own and reuse what we have. Don't throw your water bottle, plastic bag, or candy wrapper in the garbage if it can be recycled. Most towns and cities recycle paper, plastic, metal, and glass. The 3R's save money, energy, and natural resources.

Read

Read to learn more about marine wildlife and the issues that threaten their survival. Find out where they live, what they eat, and what they do each day. Find out if their ocean world is at risk and how can you help protect critical ocean habitats. Don't forget to visit your public library or swap books with friends and family.

Act

Get involved on a local level. The phrase "Think Globally, Act Locally" reminds us that we need to keep the bigger picture in mind as we work to make things better in our own communities.

Get Involved

Write letters and join organizations that work to protect our oceans. Get involved in beach cleanups and fundraising events for non-profits. Don't forget to volunteer your time and your talents.

Chat It Up

Spread the word about Salt, her life, and her ocean friends. Remind your family and friends that healthy oceans are important for the survival of humpback whales, other marine wildlife, and all life on Earth. Speak out for ocean animals and be their voice!

Choosy Consumers

When you go to the store, try to purchase items that are not overly packaged in plastic and can be reused or recycled.

Unplug and Reconnect with Nature

Turn off the TV, unplug the computer, and get outdoors! Spending time in Nature is fun, exciting, and healthy for you!

Whale Watch Field Notes

Salt

Salt and Epsom

In the spring of 2014, Salt returned with her 13th calf. Captain Chad Avellar, the son of Captain Aaron Avellar, named this little calf Epsom in honor of its famous mom. Also in 2014, Etch-A-Sketch (daughter of Thalassa and granddaughter of Salt) returned with a calf by her side. This little whale was Etch-a-Sketch's first calf and Salt's first great-granddaughter.

In the spring of 2016, Salt returned to New England waters with a calf making this her 14th offspring. Keeping with tradition, Captain Chad Avellar named the calf Sriracha. Also in 2016, three of Salt's daughters Thalassa, Mostaza, and Sanchal returned with calves as did Salt's grandchild, Etch-A-Sketch. Salt now has 14 children, 15 grandchildren and 2 great-grandchildren!

Salt Adoption Package

Adopt Salt, the humpback whale, and help support our efforts on behalf of all marine wildlife. This gift is great for kids of all ages! Each Adoption Package includes:

- a color photograph of Salt's flukes,
- a personalized certificate of adoption,
- fun fact sheets on humpback whales,
- our "Protect our Oceans" magnet,
- the DVD "Salt and Friends" by the Whale Video Company.

To adopt today, go to the NECWA website at www.necwa.org and click on our Adoption Program link.

Salt T-shirt

Our Salt t-shirt was designed by Adam Whittier and is perfect for the Salt lover in your life.

- adult unisex, stone blue
- youth unisex, blue and pink
- 6.1 oz. ultra cotton

Visit the NECWA website at www. necwa.org and learn how you can purchase your Salt t-shirt today!

Additional Notes:

To ensure accuracy, the map on page 9 was traced from a map entitled "Gerry E. Studds Stellwagen Bank National Marine Sanctuary" © 2014 NOAA, and may be viewed at stellwagen.noaa.gov/pgallery/maps.html. Similarly, the map on page 13 was traced from one by Dr. Carol Gersmehl and Debbie Bojar © 1999 Macalester College.

We wish to thank the Center for Coastal Studies for providing much of the information for Salt's family tree (www.coastalstudies.org). We also thank Plymouth & Provincetown Whale Watch for their continued support of NECWA's Internship Program (www.plymouthwhalewatching.com).

Book design, layout, and editing by Bethany Matern. Additional edits also provided by Drs. Mary Nash, Peggy Eds-Walton, and Mary Jo Danton.

Adam Whittier

Adam Whittier is a New England based cartoonist and illustrator who has done work for various publications both in print and online. His previous books include *Phoenix: the Ford Pinto Story* and *Snake Rapunzel*. To learn more about Adam and to see more of his work, go to www.adamwhittier.com.

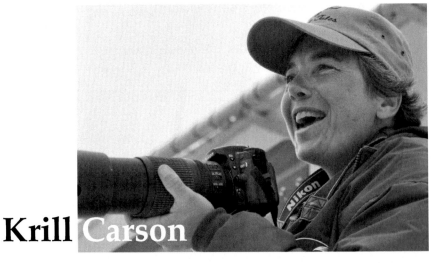

Krill Carson

Krill Carson is a marine biologist who has worked in the New England area since 1980. She received the nickname "Krill" from Captain Aaron Avellar, who also named Salt and most of her calves. In 2005, Krill founded the New England Coastal Wildlife Alliance (NECWA) and is the current President.

Made in the USA
San Bernardino, CA
03 August 2016